WINE WISDOM

WINE
WISDOM

First published in Great Britain in 1993 by Mitchell Beazley
an imprint of Reed Consumer Books Limited
Michelin House, 81 Fulham Road, London SW3 6RB
and Auckland, Melbourne, Singapore and Toronto

A CIP catalogue record for this book is available from the
British Library

ISBN 1 85732 173 1

Illustrations and jacket illustration by Conny Jude
Typeset in M Bembo
Produced by Mandarin Offset
Printed and bound in Hong Kong

Introduction

When I first took an interest in wine I read, and then tasted, whenever I could; I travelled and listened to anything and everything that I might learn from connected with wine. Certain key concepts proved their usefulness again and again.

These miscellaneous snippets were from diverse sources: friends, colleagues, books, articles, sometimes from wine merchants or growers and wine-makers themselves. The common thread was their basis in long experience in the world of wine.

In the course of my wine-writing career I have been able to set these ideas against my own experience: often they have stood the test, occasionally they have not. Now and again I have been able to add my own observations to the growing collection. I have regularly referred to this fount of wisdom while compiling my 45 or so wine books and numerous articles, when giving lectures and when advising in a personal or professional capacity.

These observations, 300 in all, are intended to be a stimulating accompaniment to any wine experience, no matter how casual. Many of the ideas collected here have spurred me on to different and better ways of approaching the subject, of choosing, serving, matching and appreciating wine, and for me this has certainly resulted in better enjoyment of it.

I humbly offer this, my collected wine wisdom, in the hope that it will enrich your experience too.

Hubrecht Duijker

If your first sip makes you long for your
second, you will know you have
discovered a good wine.

≈ ≈ ≈

Add wine,
and a meal becomes a dinner.

≈ ≈ ≈

Snobbery aside, the shape of a glass
can affect the appreciation of a wine.
It should be large enough to allow the
scent to collect above the liquid,
and clear, to show off its
'robe' or colour.

The better red Burgundies
are made exclusively from Pinot
Noir grapes.

&⁂ &⁂ &⁂

Sauvignon Blanc will happily keep
in an opened bottle for a couple of days
- especially in the refrigerator.

&⁂ &⁂ &⁂

The better the vintage, the more slowly
its red wines usually develop.

Never store wine glasses
upside down in a cupboard, as this
gives them a dusty odour.

❧ ❧ ❧

According to Italian devotees,
one barrel of wine can work more
miracles than a church full of saints.

❧ ❧ ❧

When tasting, whistle the wine
inward, making it fan out over the
whole tongue. Try this first over a large
sink - and do not be tempted
to inhale!

According to T S Eliot, all a
civilised person needs is two glasses of
Sherry before dinner.

   ❧ ❧ ❧

The aroma of gooseberries
and often asparagus can be striking in
white Sauvignon, while Pinot Noir will
suggest raspberries or even – to some –
pencil shavings.

Poor wine is always too expensive.

&a &a &a

So-called *primeur* wines from
Roussillon and Languedoc can be just as
fruity as those from Beaujolais, but are
generally much cheaper.

&a &a &a

Sherry is fortified after fermentation,
Port during. This makes Sherry's base
wine dry and Port always sweet.

Napoleon Bonaparte, one of Moët &
Chandon's more celebrated clients, was
reported to have said of Champagne:
"In victory it is deserved;
in defeat it is needed."

❧ ❧ ❧

The top classification in Burgundy
is *grand cru* followed, confusingly, by
premier cru. At least in Bordeaux,
premier cru is first in line.

The power of the Rhône's
red Gigondas has been likened to that
of a charging rhinoceros. Perhaps one to
have handy when serving a robust
stew or game dish.

It is a waste to drink any wine
too old, but don't hurry a wine that is
designed for a complex old age.

࿊ ࿊ ࿊

Outdoors, a wine can be chilled
perfectly in a stream if one can be found
nearby, but failing that, wrap a wet cloth
around the bottle and leave it in the
shade, exposed to a breeze.

Muscadet from the Loire valley goes well with many sea foods, such as fresh mussels and clams.

❧ ❧ ❧

The eighteenth-century invention of the cork changed the nature of wine completely by introducing the possibility of maturity. A good cork goes crumbly and brittle over a period of between 20 and 50 years.

A clean, factory-like cellar
with stainless steel vats and scrubbed
floor tiles probably makes better wine
than a picturesque, cobwebbed cellar
creaking with wood.

🐸 🐸 🐸

How inadequate is the term
'white wine'. Wine can be a pale straw
colour, shot with green, golden, tawny,
and a thousand shades in between
- only milk is truly white.

Wine can be judged perfectly without
actually swallowing it.

❧ ❧ ❧

Some of the raciest, steeliest, most
exciting Rieslings come from the steep,
slatey Mosel vineyards in Germany.

❧ ❧ ❧

The taste of a good wine is remembered
long after the price is forgotten.

If you can taste food, you can
taste wine, but in either case it demands
concentration, if only for
a few seconds.

    ❦ ❦ ❦

The world famous viticulture
and enology department of California
University at Davis has helped California
winemakers challenge centuries-old
European expertise.

In a restaurant, insist on pre-tasting every bottle that your table is going to have - even when it is another bottle of the same wine.

࿐ ࿐ ࿐

Sweet white Loire wines like Coteaux du Layon often need at least a decade in bottle before they show their true splendour.

࿐ ࿐ ࿐

In Australia successful, generous red wines are made from Shiraz, the Syrah of the Rhône Valley.

The first question any taster
should ask is whether he or she likes the
wine. The second question is: why?

🐌 🐌 🐌

There are six generous,
or eight perfectly adequate, glasses
to a bottle of wine.

🐌 🐌 🐌

If a wine has an aroma of
vanilla one can safely assume it was
aged in oak barrels.

White Mâcon or Mâcon-Villages is
an attractive, all-purpose wine for people
with a Burgundy preference but without
a Burgundy budget.

      ð   ð   ð

'Blanc de Blancs' on the label of a
still white wine means only that it is a
white wine made from white grapes – as
are 99 percent of all white wines.

It is harmony you should be looking for when matching wine with food.

&ea; &ea; &ea;

The intensity of a red wine's bouquet can be diminished by its being served too cold. Once in the glass, warm the wine by cupping the bowl in your hand and swirling gently.

&ea; &ea; &ea;

One of the most serious misunderstandings about restaurant wine lists is that big is necessarily good.

Over 160 communes are entitled
to call their wine 'Côtes-du-Rhône'.
About half of those can add the word
'Villages' which, like Beaujolais
Villages, implies a somewhat
superior product.

❧ ❧ ❧

Never apologise for, or be ashamed
of, your own taste in wine. Preferences
for wines vary just as much as those
for art or music.

It is quite illogical to serve
the white wine in smaller glasses
than the red.

❧ ❧ ❧

Meursault is remarkable for
being very dry and at the same time
soft and mellow. Pale gold in colour,
with a suggestion of green, its taste is
often described as 'buttery'.

Mango, passion fruit and lichee
are some of the tropical fruits that can
be present in the bouquet and taste of
Chardonnay.

❧ ❧ ❧

On Spanish wine labels, *Vino de
Crianza* means the wine has been aged
in wood. Those marked *Reserva* and
Gran Reserva have spent longer
in barrel.

Many sparkling wines of California
have the lightness, the delicacy and the
true racing bubble at about a half
the price of Champagne.

಄ ಄ ಄

Alsace wines are not known,
as all German wines and most French
wines are, by the names of regions or
villages: they are named after the grape
variety from which they are made
(though sometimes a vineyard
can be mentioned too).

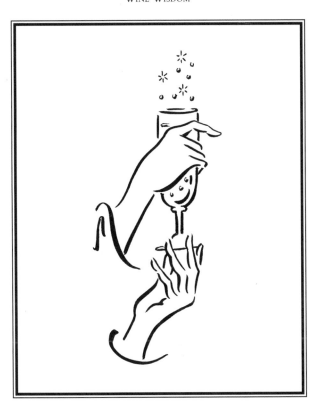

The wide use of Cabernet Sauvignon, Chardonnay and other French grapes makes Bulgaria the France of Eastern Europe.

ἐ▲ ἐ▲ ἐ▲

Spanish red wines with a large proportion of Tempranillo - like Ribera del Duero and many Riojas - keep easily for a day or two in an opened bottle.

Oregon produces some of the world's best red wines from the notoriously difficult Pinot Noir.

❧ ❧ ❧

While those in favour of decanting argue that an old wine needs to breathe for anything from a few minutes to a few days to reach its best, others hold that decanting long in advance does nothing but harm, tiring the wine and dulling the brilliance of its bouquet.

Almost all restaurants in Beaujolais serve *coq au vin* with the local wine. It is an unbeatable combination.

ôô ôô ôô

There are only 80-odd miles dividing the similar-sounding regions of Pouilly-Fuissé and Pouilly-Fumé, but the wines themselves should not be confused. The Fuissé (made from Chardonnay) is gentle and generous, while the Fumé (from Sauvignon) is fresher and crisper.

The best Chilean Sauvignon
Blancs can now challenge the more
expensive Loire wines.

❧ ❧ ❧

As a rule of thumb, the longer the
aftertaste, the better the wine.

❧ ❧ ❧

Swirl a concentrated, fat, alcoholic
wine around your glass and it will form
clearly visible 'legs' or streaks that linger
as they slide down.

If a cork is immovable, hold the
neck of the bottle briefly under warm
water to expand the glass a little.

🐌 🐌 🐌

Wine is the intellectual part of the meal.

🐌 🐌 🐌

Ideally, the temperature in a
cellar should be maintained at a constant
11°C (52°F): the perfect serving
temperature for many whites.

A true Chablis should have a
cool, mineral-like tone, and be fresh
and appetising.

🐦 🐦 🐦

Of all hocks, those from the
Rheingau can have the greatest finesse.

🐦 🐦 🐦

With cheese, a dry white wine,
especially from the Chardonnay grape,
can taste as good as - sometimes better
than - a red.

There is often less difference between
Bordeaux and Bordeaux Supérieur than
the label would indicate.

🐦 🐦 🐦

Enormous investment in the best
modern equipment, and vast plantings of
the classic vine varieties have catapulted
Bulgaria into the ranks of the quality
wine countries. Bulgarian Cabernet
Sauvignon and Chardonnay are
still staggering value.

Wine without alcohol is like
music without bass.

ða ða ða

Spicy, succulent Gewurztraminer
from Alsace is one of the few dry white
wines that can be served perfectly after a
red wine, with the cheese.

ða ða ða

As with many art forms, the
more you know about wine, the
more you enjoy it.

An opened bottle of sweet, slightly fortified, Muscat from southern France will keep for weeks if stored in the refrigerator.

ðə ðə ðə

The best moments for sparkling wines are spontaneous ones.

ðə ðə ðə

For an unusual but refreshing summer combination, try pouring some ripe red Bordeaux over fresh strawberries.

If you have one or more cases of a
wine maturing, try a bottle once in a
while to check its progress.

❧ ❧ ❧

Australian wine labels, front and back,
are generally extremely informative.
This practice should serve as an
example for other countries.

❧ ❧ ❧

Remember that the notion of serving
wine at 'room temperature' dates from a
time when central heating was not
the norm.

Few white wines exist in such
variety as Vouvray from the Loire. It
boasts dry, semi-dry, sweet, still, pétillant
and sparkling versions.

≈ ≈ ≈

Dry white Port should be
drunk ice-cold.

≈ ≈ ≈

A waiter or waitress should show
you the label before you taste the wine
simply to confirm that you have been
brought what you ordered.

The most boring of bores
is a wine bore.

&a &a &a

Always make notes, no matter how
short, about wines you like.

&a &a &a

Even château owners cannot always
recognise their own wine at blind
tastings – so why should you?

The fewer treatments a wine undergoes, the more backbone and character it normally has.

a a a

The driest type of Madeira is Sercial, the sweetest – and the original – is Malmsey.

a a a

When planning a festive dinner with friends, reckon on one bottle per person, counting all the different wines together.

Israel's best wines come from
the Golan Heights which, unlike
most Israeli vineyards, is sited away
from the savage summer heat
of the coastal plain.

ঞ ঞ ঞ

Little distinguishes Coteaux du
Tricastin wines from their Côtes du
Rhône neighbours, except their
appreciably lower prices.

A glass of Amontillado Sherry
can be an agreeable companion to
a variety of soups.

a a a

A humid cellar destroys labels.
Hair spray or cellophane wrap
provide some protection.

a a a

Saumur is not only a white and
a red wine, but also a very pleasant,
reasonably-priced sparkler.

White wines can be made
from black grapes by fermenting the
juice separately from the skins.

❧ ❧ ❧

Swirling, sloshing and spitting
at wine tastings is not considered
impolite – these are all vital elements
of the tasters' craft.

❧ ❧ ❧

The seaside hills of La Clape in
the Coteaux du Languedoc produce
agreeable red, rosé and distinctive
white wines.

Lamb is a good partner
not only for red Bordeaux but for red
Rioja, Navarra, Ribera del Duero and
Chianti - among others!

ཟ ཟ ཟ

Alentejo in Portugal, formerly
provenance of the world's best quality
corks, is being 'discovered' as a new
wine growing area, and beginning
to produce some good,
everyday reds.

Precise description of tastes and
smells can be well-nigh impossible:
one sip senses more than
a thousand words.

৯ ৯ ৯

Even the most subtle differences
between wines are perceptible when
tasting them comparatively.

৯ ৯ ৯

The lightest, freshest, most delicate
Muscadets are bottled 'sur lie', that is
directly from the cask, without
having been racked.

The whole of Bulgaria, except
the countryside around the capital
Sofia, has been declared a wine growing
area. The country is now one of the
world's largest exporters of
bottled wines.

⁂

The ten or 20 years specified on
the label of a Tawny Port mean that the
wines used in it have this average age.
Most of that time will have
been spent in casks.

The quality of Chilean wines has increased far more quickly than their price, which explains in part their phenomenal success.

☙ ☙ ☙

In 1877, when composing his Parsifal in Bayreuth, Wagner urgently ordered 100 bottles of Saint-Péray, apparently to help lubricate the creative process.

To a cynic, a great deal of
wine-speak hyperbole is 'noble rot',
but watch the cynic turn zealot after
tasting the sweet, opulent, golden-green
wines of Sauternes.

છે. છે. છે.

Australia's intensely fruity Chardonnays
and its best Cabernets, lavishly seasoned
with oak, can compete with any French
or California equivalent.

Dry white Frascati, soft, faintly nutty and full of charm, comes from the Alban Hills near Rome. It goes well with many pasta and fish dishes.

🐸 🐸 🐸

Tannin, extracted from the grapes' stalks, skins and pips and from the barrel during maturation, is the stuff that clings to your teeth. It gives red wine ageing potential and greater stability.

Strangely - and quite erroneously - the quality of the Bordeaux vintage is often seen as an indicator of the quality of all the world's regions.

ð& ð& ð&

Crémant is a term of quality - replacing the old *mousseux* - for some of the best French sparkling wines. Of the various types, Crémant de Bourgogne is one fine French alternative to Champagne.

Before tasting, smell the empty glass
to make sure it has no odour of its own
from storage boxes, detergents
or whatever.

🐸 🐸 🐸

The scent of Gamay often calls to mind
raspberries, cherries, strawberries and
other small red fruits.

When tasting, first impressions are
often the most revealing.

ટ&ล ટ&ล ટ&ล

Rheinpfalz is the sunniest and
driest wine region of Germany, which
is reflected in its soft white wines.

ટ&ล ટ&ล ટ&ล

Complexity is what you pay for - and
hope to savour - in most great wines.

Fresh, fruity and aromatic, Sancerre is a perfect partner for goat's cheese. Try it with Crottin de Chavignol, from the Sancerre region itself.

❧ ❧ ❧

Colour is the first indicator of a red wine's age. The wine runs out of the fermentation vat deep blackish-purple, and from that moment on it gently fades and browns.

Beaujolais produces more wine
than all four other Burgundy districts
put together.

⁂

With Barolo - one of Italy's most
muscular reds - all the flavour and most
of the extraordinary spectrum of scents
are masked for several years. Maturity
begins develop after about ten years.

A good Crozes-Hermitage
represents excellent value for money.
Its grape is the noble black Syrah, which
provides such other classics as
Hermitage and Côte Rôtie.

≈ ≈ ≈

The rating of a vintage can never
be more than a crude average, a global
estimate, the highest common factor of a
particular year's quality.

Sediment in a wine is natural and harmless. Careful pouring and decanting will eliminate the problem.

❧ ❧ ❧

Joseph Dargent, a rather appropriately named spokesman for Champagne, once wrote that no government could survive without his product, it being the oil of the diplomatic machine.

❧ ❧ ❧

Some of the Médoc's better crus bourgeois can match the classified growths.

If someone wants to give you
a vintage wine to celebrate your
birthday - make sure you were born
in a great year!

&a &a &a

One of the least-known and
most remarkable dry Loire wines is the
splendid, powerful, long-lived
Savennières from
west of Angers.

The climate and soil in
South Africa give it the potential
to make wines comparable with any in
the New World, and even
perhaps the Old.

⁂ ⁂ ⁂

Stainless steel vats are commonplace
for fermenting white wines because
temperature control is easier, but new
oak barrels are increasingly favoured
for high quality wines.

White Zinfandel or blush
wine from California is in fact a
semi-sweet rosé.

🐸 🐸 🐸

If you make a speculative
investment in wine as a commodity,
you run the risk of turning a relaxing,
delicious product into a financial
nightmare.

🐸 🐸 🐸

White Menetou-Salon is almost
identical to Sancerre, but usually costs
a little less.

Before decanting an old wine,
remove the whole capsule. You can
then see the sediment better as you
pour.

🐌 🐌 🐌

Perhaps the most frustrating truth
for wine collectors is that one knows
only in retrospect when a wine
was at its peak.

🐌 🐌 🐌

The two red giants of the Rhône valley
are Côte Rôtie and Hermitage.

Vinegar, hot mustard, curry
and pungent spices are some of wine's
worst enemies.

❧ ❧ ❧

A top-quality Sauternes is a fine partner
for fresh Roquefort.

❧ ❧ ❧

In the refreshing whites from
Alto Adige in north-eastern Italy
you can almost taste the clean
mountain air.

Look out for the second wines from classified Bordeaux growths. They can be excellent value for money.

ٿ ٿ ٿ

Robert Louis Stevenson – who honeymooned in Napa – thought of wine as bottled poetry.

ٿ ٿ ٿ

Chilean Cabernet Sauvignon can prove better value than a red Bordeaux of the same price.

When opening Champagne,
remove the foil and wire muzzle but
keep a finger and thumb on the cork.
Ease this out by slowly turning the
bottle, holding it at an angle. Have
the glasses ready before you
begin and ... enjoy!

❧ ❧ ❧

Ice and water in a bucket
chill a bottle much more quickly than
ice alone. A spoonful of salt speeds up
the process, which can take ten times as
long if the bottle is simply put in
the refrigerator.

What is green about Portugal's white
Vinho Verde is its spring-like freshness.

The most typical Austrian wine is made from the popular white Grüner Veltliner and has a dry, almost peppery bite.

🐌 🐌 🐌

Alsace is one of the few regions that make Muscat grapes into dry wine. The aroma is almost sweet but the flavour is light, fruity and clean – an excellent choice as an apéritif.

If a sweet wine is served at the
beginning of a meal, a clear soup to
follow will clean the palate for
the drier wines.

ॐ ॐ ॐ

Some California winemakers
maintain that they are not there to make
money but to pursue a dream: the only
way to make a small fortune in the
wine business is, apparently, to
start with a large one.

Apart from Soave, two other whites
from around Verona worth seeking out
are Bianco di Custoza and Lugana.

&. &. &.

The names of Alsatian wines,
villages, vineyards and growers may
sound German, but the region is
wholeheartedly French.

&. &. &.

Many Chilean wine cellars are
just as well equipped as their European,
Australian and American counterparts.

White, sweetish Graves
Supérieures is in fact the most inferior
wine produced in the Graves district.

❧ ❧ ❧

Always check to make certain that
the poured wine is clear.

❧ ❧ ❧

Up to 13 different grape varieties
can be used in a single blend to achieve
the concentrated flavour that is red
Châteauneuf-du-Pape.

The quality of a vintage is usually
determined in the last few weeks - or
even days - before the harvest.

⁂

New Zealand's white Sauvignons are
dry, fresh and stimulating - and among
the very best in the world.

⁂

Small crystals in the bottle or on
the bottom of the cork are usually
tartrate crystals, natural in wine,
flavourless and harmless.

Few dessert wines are so complicated to make, so light and so deliciously aromatic as Moscato d'Asti from Italy.

❧ ❧ ❧

Good wine deserves good food - and vice versa. So don't economise on one if you haven't on the other.

❧ ❧ ❧

Lalande-de-Pomerol, made north of the Pomerol boundary, is at its best certainly of junior Pomerol class, but will cost a third or so less than the original.

Hosts and hostesses might also
profit from the restaurateurs' maxim: as
apéritifs, Port relaxes while
Sherry excites.

❧ ❧ ❧

Affordable reds from Bordeaux
varieties are the speciality of Moldova
in Eastern Europe.

❧ ❧ ❧

Wine, as the Dutch poet Werumeus
Buning once observed, is the flower in
the buttonhole of civilisation.

The sturdy, red Bulgarian wine made
from Melnik goes well with spicy,
robust dishes and strong cheese. Locals
claim it is so concentrated that you can
carry it in a handkerchief.

Pinot Grigio from Grave del Friuli
or Alto Adige is a soft but refreshing
white wine, full of charm and
ideal for summer.

🐌 🐌 🐌

There is little evidence that a
smoker's tasting abilities are any less
discerning than a non-smoker's: many
reputable tasters are smokers - some
even light up a strong French
cigarette between
tasting sessions.

Red wines from Sonoma County,
California, tend to be somewhat softer
than those from neighbouring Napa.

ə. ə. ə.

Gewurztraminer is much the
most easily recognisable one-wine grape:
its special spicy aroma epitomises
Alsace wine.

ə. ə. ə.

Beaujolais Primeur may not be offered
for sale before the third Thursday of the
November in its harvest year.

Let the taste of the wine
determine whether or not you like it:
not its reputation or price.

🍂 🍂 🍂

Mistrust a young, *dry* white wine that
shows a golden or brownish colour, but
remember that sweet Sauternes can be
deep gold and still be in its youth.

🍂 🍂 🍂

Malbec is a typical Argentinean red wine
grape: in the bottle it combines fruit and
spice into an attractive whole.

Most of the best Chianti
comes from the Classico area south of
Florence, where bottles are sealed with a
black rooster, badge of the *Consorzio
Vino Chianti Classico*.

🐦 🐦 🐦

New Zealand has what many Australian
and California winemakers can only
dream of: growing conditions that
almost guarantee slowly-ripened,
highly aromatic fruit.

Decant an old wine in one
continuous movement, over a light
source, and stop pouring as soon as
sediment approaches the
bottle neck.

❧ ❧ ❧

The slightly fortified Muscats
from southern France - Frontignan
is the biggest and best-known - are
dependable, all-purpose
dessert wines.

A classic - and appetising
- combination from Alsace is
Gewurztraminer with the regional
Munster cheese.

&. &. &.

'There are only two occasions
when I drink Champagne,' averred
S D Churchill, in *All Sorts and Condition
of Drinks* , 'and those are when I have
game for dinner, and
when I haven't.'

In principle every individual wine producer makes the wine he or she likes best: the winemaker's taste determines that of the wine.

ತ್ತ ತ್ತ ತ್ತ

Some light white wines have a tiny prickle - a *pétillance* - in their taste. It is built into the wine to keep it tasting extra fresh.

Sauternes is rarely sweet
enough to accompany a sweet dessert,
but combines perfectly with fresh
peaches, pears and apricots.

In spite of the vogue for built-in
wine racks in fashionable new kitchens,
the wildly varying temperatures that
occur in that room make it
probably the least sensible
place to store wine.

ﷺ ﷺ ﷺ

A Nebbiolo d'Alba can be seen as
a poor man's Barolo: it has none of the
latter's stern majesty, but can develop a
delicious bouquet of fruit ranging
from plums to raspberries.

Riesling from Alsace is a
safe choice as an accompaniment
to many fish dishes.

🐌 🐌 🐌

Vintage Port always throws
a sediment (called the 'crust') but other
single harvest Ports, like Late Bottled
Vintage and Colheita, do not.

🐌 🐌 🐌

Almost any wine, if thoughtfully chosen,
makes a perfect Valentine.

Canada, Lebanon and
Luxembourg are lesser-known wine
countries where delicious discoveries
can be made.

🐦 🐦 🐦

Madeira is one of the
most useful wines to have in the
kitchen. One of the drier varieties, such
as Verdelho, enhances the flavour of
many dishes and, even after the bottle
has been opened, keeps its flavour
for weeks, especially if kept in
the refrigerator.

Treat an old wine
as you would an old person:
with care and respect.

&a &a &a

The delicious taste of
asparagus demands a carefully chosen
accompaniment, such as Pinot Blanc
(Alsace), Sauvignon de Touraine,
Sancerre, Menetou-Salon, Quincy,
Reuilly or Pouilly-Fumé.

&a &a &a

The Italian version of a *primeur*
wine is *vino novello*.

Always store wine bottles
on their side to prevent their corks
from drying out.

ર~ ર~ ર~

If it's a red Dão, the name stands for
a firm, sturdy, usually inexpensive wine
from Portugal.

ર~ ર~ ર~

Fino and Manzanilla Sherries are
perfect with *tapas*, the infinitely various
Spanish savoury snacks.

In modern winemaking
the role of chance is diminishing as that
of technique grows - which is good
news for the consumer.

❧ ❧ ❧

Some Italian DOC wines are further
categorised as DOCG. The additional
'G' stands for *Garantita*, the implication
being that such wines are officially
guaranteed as Italy's best. Sadly,
the implication does not always
match the truth.

The white wines
from America's second wine state,
Washington, are generally more elegant
and fragrant than those of California.

෨ ෨ ෨

Chocolate is a notoriously difficult
taste to marry with wine, but the dark
nectars of Spanish Málaga and Pedro
Ximénez can be delicious with
chocolate desserts.

Muscadet should be drunk
as young as possible.

❧ ❧ ❧

Young red Rioja without barrel ageing
can be a splendid wine: deep purple,
meaty and bursting with fruit.

❧ ❧ ❧

Heavily tannic wines are often
much more approachable when
accompanied by food.

In the last 20 years
the quality of Spanish wines has
improved more than it did in the
preceding 20 centuries.

≈ ≈ ≈

Tokay Pinot Gris from Alsace can be
recognised by its somewhat smoky
bouquet and taste.

≈ ≈ ≈

Champagne is the perfect appetiser – as
are all other quality dry sparklers.

A great wine becomes a reference point
- perhaps for the rest of your life.

❧ ❧ ❧

Pouilly-Fumé tends to taste somewhat
firmer than Sancerre, and demands a
little more patience.

❧ ❧ ❧

Good Beaujolais *en primeur* can still
be delicious at Easter - but why
wait so long?

Chianti needs to be selected carefully, for there are many styles and qualities on the market.

        🐦   🐦   🐦

Liebfraumilch accounts for about half of Germany's total wine export.

        🐦   🐦   🐦

Train yourself to compare every wine with the best of that kind you have ever tasted.

Benjamin Franklin's attractive
philosophy was: wine furnishes constant
proof that God loves us, and loves
to see us happy.

ða ða ða

Red Graves
could be characterised as a softer
version of Médoc.

ða ða ða

Wine from organically grown vines
is usually more expensive than regular
wine - and not necessarily better.

The old saying 'buy on apples and sell on cheese' still applies, as cheese will flatter wine, while a bite of apple will cleanse and sharpen the palate, allowing an unbiased judgement.

Of all red Loire wines, one of the finest - perfect with red meat - is Chinon. The best wines from the best vintages also have ageing potential.

Too many wine writers
place wine on a pedestal instead of
on the table.

Sediment in a bottle is mainly
tannin from the wine itself.

❧ ❧ ❧

White Beaujolais can be
surprisingly delicious.

❧ ❧ ❧

A refreshing, affordable apéritif
or salad wine is the light white Vin de
Pays des Côtes de Gascogne from
Southwest France.

In the white Muscadet region the
largest and best district is Muscadet de
Sèvre et Maine.

⁂

The sun's ultraviolet rays and
most neon lamps have the effect of
ageing wine prematurely, so watch out
for bottles that may have been exposed
to this kind of light for some time.

If you have a complaint
regarding your wine in a restaurant, ask
the waiter, waitress or maître d'hôtel
to taste the wine for themselves.

ða   ða   ða

The biggest winery
in the world is Gallo in Modesto,
California. It is said to produce about
one million cases per week, and has its
own glass factory.

Before decanting a wine, make sure
that the carafe is totally clean and has no
trace of any smell.

🍂 🍂 🍂

One could almost fancy a Banyuls
from Roussillon to be a well-judged
combination of Port and Madeira.

🍂 🍂 🍂

By the quality of a house wine
you can usually judge the quality of the
restaurant's wine list; and a good wine
list normally means a good kitchen.

The most elegant Médocs are usually
those of Margaux, the firmest
those of St Estèphe.

❧ ❧ ❧

Einstein would have loved it: at a wine
tasting, everything is relative.

❧ ❧ ❧

A pleasant, affordable alternative for red
Bordeaux is oak-aged Buzet.

South Africa's most planted
variety is the Chenin Blanc (called Steen
locally) but keep an eye open for good
Sauvignon Blancs and Chardonnays.

🐛 🐛 🐛

Choose a Burgundy first and foremost
on the reputation of its producer.

🐛 🐛 🐛

A typical California grape is the black
Zinfandel, which can give meaty red
wines with spicy rich fruit.

The sermon of moderation
has ancient origins: Ecclesiasticus
held that wine was created from the
beginning to make men joyful, not to
make them drunk.

≥ ≥ ≥

The older the vine the fewer grapes
it yields, but those grapes have more
quality potential than grapes
from young plants.

The best Mosel and Rhine wines
from great vintages can age just as well
as tannic red wines.

ن ن ن

Manzanilla is the speciality sherry
of Sanlúcar de Barrameda. Matured in
bodegas by the sea, it takes on an almost
salty tang that makes it more than
usually appetising. With some
more barrel age it becomes
a Manzanilla Pasada.

All the best white Burgundies
are based on the Chardonnay grape.

෪ ෪ ෪

It takes on average one hundred days
for a vine's flowers to develop
into ripe grapes.

෪ ෪ ෪

It is usually better to serve younger,
lighter wines before older, firmer ones.

Leftover wine can be used to add
richness to numerous sweet and savoury
dishes. It can take the place of lemon
juice or vinegar in salad dressings
or, mixed with oil and herbs, be
used to tenderise and flavour
dry meat in a marinade.

❧ ❧ ❧

Marsala, known to the Sicilians as
'English wine', was originally created by
an English pharmaceutical salesman in
the middle of the eighteenth century. It
exists in sweet and dry versions.

It is the very last sip of a great wine
that usually tastes the best.

❧ ❧ ❧

Of all Eastern European countries
Hungary – cradle of the legendary
Tokay – probably has the greatest
quality potential.

❧ ❧ ❧

Dry Sherry benefits from being served as
cool as any other white wine.

A clean, empty milk bottle is the
world's cheapest decanter.

The greatest Burgundies, red or white, come from the 'golden slopes' of the Côte d'Or - but this name never appears on the label.

❧ ❧ ❧

About a third of all Greek wine has pine-resin added, and is called Retsina. The wine, likened by some to high quality furniture polish, goes well with Greek cooking but is initially a fairly marked departure from non-Greek tastes.

George Washington stated that his living was plain: a glass of wine and a leg of mutton were always at hand.

❧ ❧ ❧

Top Australian Chardonnays are now accepted as world class.

❧ ❧ ❧

All kinds of Beaujolais benefit from being served cooler than other red wines.

Vintage Madeira is kept in cask for at least 20 years before bottling. It is still then deemed a young wine and needs another 20 to 50 years in bottle to become sublime.

❧ ❧ ❧

The *Cavas* of Penedès range from the extremely deft and delicate to the mediocre and clumsy, but the best can certainly be counted among the world's top sparkling wines.

It was Johann Strauss who linked a waltz and a glass of wine as two of life's great pleasures that invite their own encore.

ᓂ ᓂ ᓂ

The language of wine is just as necessary as that of music.

ᓂ ᓂ ᓂ

Saint-Véran is appealing as a somewhat lighter and less costly version of Pouilly-Fuissé.

Most sweet after-dinner wines profit
from spending half an hour in
the refrigerator.

🐌 🐌 🐌

In Sauternes, harvesting machines
are eschewed in favour of discerning
human pickers who make several *tries* or
passages through the vineyard, picking
individual grapes at just the right
moment, and leaving others on
the vine to become more
concentrated in sugar.

Dry white Torrontés from Argentina has
a seductive, Muscat-like aroma.

&. &. &.

Thomas Jefferson remarked that no
nation is drunk where
wine is cheap.

&. &. &.

White wine that is fermented in new
oak barrels offers more dimensions than
that which is not - but at a price.

According to legend, the Champagne 'coupe', the wide, shallow glass on a stem, was modelled on the bosom of Marie-Antoinette.

❧ ❧ ❧

In an historic tasting in Paris in 1976 a range of French and California wines was offered in unmarked bottles. In both groups, red and white, the distinguished French judges were horrified to discover that they had pronounced California wines the best.

As Philippe de Rothschild said,
with today's knowledge of wine and
winemaking there are no more
'bad' years, only 'greater' and
'lighter' vintages.

🐾 🐾 🐾

Unlike a film or a book, wine is
constantly evolving, so wine criticism,
no matter how authoritative, can never
be definitive, but applies only
to a limited period.

Many of the best red and
white wines from the Graves district of
Bordeaux are not called Graves, but
Pessac-Léognan.

❧ ❧ ❧

Champagne has many more uses than
just an apéritif. HM Queen Elizabeth II
set a royal example when she offered
President Reagan and company Pol
Roger 1969 with fresh rasperries
at Windsor Castle in 1982.

The choice of grape has an enormous influence on the wine's ageability. Small grapes with thick skins and high pip-to-juice ratios are most likely to produce wines that develop and last.

&. &. &.

Italian *classico* wines are made in the heart of their zone which is, by implication, the oldest and usually the best part.

Red Port was a creation of the British,
and - some say - tastes best with
English Stilton cheese.

❧ ❧ ❧

The truth is not on the label
- but behind it.

❧ ❧ ❧

South African Pinotage, made from
a cross between Pinot Noir and Cinsaut,
can be very exciting, or extremely
dull - so choose carefully.

A 'corked' wine
has a chlorine-like, foul aroma.

☙ ☙ ☙

Many would regard as prophetic
the fact that the Rothschild family and
other eminent French winemakers have
invested in Chilean wine estates.

☙ ☙ ☙

Good wine does not have to be
expensive.

The language at Bulgaria's wine university in Plovdiv is French. It shows which country serves as its model.

❧ ❧ ❧

Dear friends merit dear wines.

❧ ❧ ❧

Complex soils produce complex wines. This is one of the secrets of the great reds of Médoc.

Find a wine supplier you can trust
- and stay faithful to him.

ε₂ ε₂ ε₂

Austria's sweet white Ausleses are
normally less expensive than comparable
wines from Germany.

ε₂ ε₂ ε₂

A good Soave has been described as
Vivaldi in your glass.

The smaller the bottle, the more
quickly the wine matures.

ཨ ཨ ཨ

At least 75 percent of the world's
wine is probably meant to be drunk
within a year of being made.

ཨ ཨ ཨ

Judge the colour of a wine by tilting
the glass against a white background.

'Horizontal' and 'vertical'
tastings are not so-called after the
tasters' angle of incline at the end of the
day – they describe the method of wine
selection. Horizontal tastings compare
wines from different places but of the
same vintage; vertical tastings
compare different vintages
of the same wine.

❧ ❧ ❧

Perhaps the best white Sauvignons
from the whole of Southwest France are
those from Côtes de Duras.

The Russian author Gorki
once described a red wine as bottled
solar energy

*& *& *&

A 'corked' wine can seldom be
detected by sniffing the cork alone. You
really need to smell or taste the
wine to be sure.

*& *& *&

Too many sommeliers see it as a
professional challenge to keep 'their'
bottles out of the guests' reach.

Wine is the most civilised thing in the world, according to Ernest Hemingway

🐌 🐌 🐌

Less than ten of Australia's
550 or so producers bottle two thirds
of the country's wine.

🐌 🐌 🐌

A polite description of even the most
horrible wine is 'interesting'.

Life is far too short
to drink bad wine.